CRM

in a week

NAOMI LANGFORD-WOOD
BRIAN SALTER

Hodder & Stoughton

A MEMBER OF THE HODDER HEADLINE GROUP

Orders: please contact Bookpoint Ltd, 130 Milton Park, Abingdon, Oxon
OX14 4SB.
Telephone: (44) 01235 827720, Fax: (44) 01235 400454. Lines are open from
9.00–6.00, Monday to Saturday, with a 24-hour message answering service.
E-mail address: orders@bookpoint.co.uk

British Library Cataloguing in Publication Data
A catalogue record for this title is available from The British Library

ISBN 0 340 857668

First published	2002
Impression number	10 9 8 7 6 5 4 3 2 1
Year	2007 2006 2005 2004 2003 2002

Typeset by SX Composing DTP, Rayleigh, Essex.
Printed in Great Britain for Hodder & Stoughton Educational, a division of
Hodder Headline Plc, 338 Euston Road, London NW1 3BH by
Cox & Wyman Ltd., Reading.

The leading organisation for professional management

As the champion of management, the Chartered Management Institute shapes and supports the managers of tomorrow. By sharing intelligent insights and setting standards in management development, the Institute helps to deliver results in a dynamic world.

Setting and raising standards

The Institute is a nationally accredited organisation, responsible for setting standards in management and recognising excellence through the award of professional qualifications.

Encouraging development, improving performance

The Institute has a vast range of development programmes, qualifications, information resources and career guidance to help managers and their organisations meet new challenges in a fast-changing environment.

Shaping opinion

With in-depth research and regular policy surveys of its 91,000 individual members and 520 corporate members, the Chartered Management Institute has a deep understanding of the key issues. Its view is informed, intelligent and respected.

For more information call 01536 204222 or visit www.managers.org.uk

C O N T E N T S

To see the way that some businesses are run, you would think that customers are the last thing they really want. Customers, as we all know, are tyrants and life would be much easier without having to pander to their every whim. Unfortunately however, it is a fundamental fact of corporate life that without customers there would be no revenues and, therefore, by definition no business.

To misquote the old bard:

> *Some people are born to manage customers; some achieve customer manager status whilst others have CRM thrust upon them.*

Finding new customers and retaining existing clients is really the only game in town for all businesses. Building loyal, long-term customer relationships is one of the main prerequisites for corporate survival.

The promise of customer relationship management is captivating, and the corporate winners will be those who put their customers at the very apex of everything they do.

We have written this book as an incentive to encourage managers at all levels to commit to their customers – both internal and external – over and above everything else that they strive to do. Every day you will be considering a different aspect of CRM, and by the end of the week you will have covered:

• **Sunday**	What CRM is
• **Monday**	The customer
• **Tuesday**	Channels to the customer
• **Wednesday**	Call centres and help desks
• **Thursday**	Company culture
• **Friday**	Motivation
• **Saturday**	Implementation

Whether you are a manager in a large organisation, or you are a sole-trader, you can simply take the concepts outlined in this book and apply them to your own situation. You have nothing to lose and almost everything to gain. Good planning and good luck!

What is CRM?

Mention those magic words Customer Relationship Management or CRM, to a number of different people and you might be surprised at the number of definitions you get.

Some will tell you that it is a way of computerising your business. Others will spell out a series of techniques and tools to deal with your customers. Yet others will tell you it is all about marketing to individuals. Supermarket gurus may tell you that it is all about loyalty schemes. Service industries will say 'Don't forget the help desks' or 'How about a relational database for key account management?'

In a way they are all right, but they only provide a glimpse of what all the fuss is about and they only focus on one aspect of the whole. In fact, all of these points are sticking-plasters on the whole plan.

CRM has come in vogue over the last few years, yet the ideas behind CRM are not new. However, with the advent of newer technologies – especially the arrival of the internet – many of the ideas that would have been prohibitively expensive to put into practice just a decade ago, suddenly become achievable.

CRM is simply a means of building individual relationships with your customers, way beyond the numbers with whom you could have hoped to have one-to-one or quality relationships with before. Although the new technologies enable this process, CRM is not solely to do with the new breed of IT applications and integrating systems. On their own they are not so useful. They need something else – a far more fundamental business issue.

CRM is a philosophy; it is about creating a revolution in the way that business is done throughout the company. It describes a strategy that places the customer at the very heart of everything the company does.

CRM recognises that each and every one of your customers are individuals with their own needs, aspirations and desires. By recognising customers as individuals, an organisation can start treating them in the way *they* would wish to be treated, and not as just another punter waiting to be dealt with at arms-length.

Consider hairdressing salons, for a moment. Some hairdressers command extraordinary loyalty from their customers. Many people insist on going to one particular stylist and will accept no other in the salon. Even if they move house, the customer will often drive miles just to revisit that same hairdresser. Now, that hairdresser does not have unique skills. Nevertheless, successful salons have learned

that looking after their customers, as well as having clean premises, good coffee and other drinks, attention to detail, a broad selection of magazines and generally pampering their customers to make them feel good about themselves, will amply reward their investment in time and costs. In principle it is the same as the major cosmetic houses who create a 'me-too factor' and 'I'm worth it' philosophy with their packaging. This is aimed fairly and squarely at their chosen target market and it works extremely well.

So, what's new?

Isn't CRM just a new fad to describe something that we have all aspired to for many years?

Well, actually, no. In the past, the traditional role of marketing has focused on key marketing elements such as:

- Product description
- Price points
- Promotional activities
- Placement

It has not focused on relationship marketing. Traditional marketing is still relevant and needs addressing, just as it always did. However, what CRM adds to this mix is not only the necessity of winning new customers, but also of keeping your existing customers so happy that they keep coming back for more of your products or services, as well as being so happy that they sing your praises and recommend your firm to others.

CRM is all about establishing long-term relationships. To do this effectively, a company will begin to 'own' its customers and thereby improve customer retention and profitability for the company.

In order to deliver maximum satisfaction to increasing numbers of customers, information needs to be gathered about them which can then be used strategically; not only with existing customers but also to build up your suspects and prospects. At the same time, associates, partners and employees will need to be 'in on the act' to gain the exponential growth curve in revenues that you want.

Customers' loyalty can be won – or lost – depending on how you deal with them and whether they get what they want. CRM is not a magic bullet and it certainly cannot be implemented in a piecemeal fashion. It simply will not work that way.

This means not leaving it with the IT department and then blaming them when it fails to deliver. After all, that is only focusing on part of the solution – IT or technology. It needs to be systemic throughout all business systems and CRM should, therefore, be a planned initiative from the board throughout the company. For make no mistake, CRM is nothing short of a revolution in the way that the company works and thinks. It cannot be driven by the IT department and certainly not simply by the use of newly installed technology. No. It is essential that all CRM is strategically driven if real benefits are to be produced. Without that, the business will end up tripping over itself because parts of it will be grossly out of sync with other parts.

So where do we start?

Many companies have long operated some sort of CRM, even if they have never called it that. For instance, placing an '0800 Helpline' sticker on the back of an appliance might be seen as being customer-focused. It certainly adds a comfort factor to end users and lets them know that they have not been left with no apparent support.

In fact, the 0800 syndrome has even stretched to the placing of a phone number on the back of delivery vehicles with a message, such as *'How am I driving? Ring 0800…'* The idea, of course, is to emphasise to other road users that the company actually cares about the impression that its delivery men give to the general public. Mind you, have you ever even attempted, or do you know of anyone else, who has actually tried ringing that number? The customer management gurus within companies might be a little less complacent if they just tried it once in a while! In our experience, too many companies dismiss the caller with empty excuses. Sadly, these kind of piecemeal offerings often give the appearance of sea change when nothing else has actually happened within the company – similar to putting an alarm box on the outside of a building without installing the rest of the system or wiring it up.

But this approach to CRM is only scratching the surface. A four-stage approach is needed:

1 *Analysis*: a company-wide review of what information is held about customers, products and services, and what is needed or desired. Then the data collection can be set up properly in the first place.

2 *Integration*: a pooling of information about customers from all the different channels the company uses. We will look at channels on Tuesday.

3 *Updating*: in order to avoid customers repeating their details whenever they place a new order or when transferred from one company employee to another, details need to be captured and kept up to date.

4 *Anticipation*: companies need to use the information they have gathered to anticipate demand. Ideally, by having a record of a customer's trading history, they should be able to forecast what products and services the customer is likely to buy in the future, and – perhaps equally as important – what goods they will not want.

Some everyday examples of CRM in practice

- Low-cost airlines such as Ryanair, Easyjet, Go! and Buzz give their customers instant access via the internet to timetables and tariffs. They allow people to book their tickets online which are then simply printed out on the customers' printer. By identifying regular customers, these airlines can offer targeted deals to individuals and encourage them to make better use of their flights and earn substantial savings. The companies offer special loyalty deals to encourage customers to continue using their airline instead of going to a competitor next time. At the time of writing Go! even prints an invitation from its chief executive, Barbara Cassini, in its in-flight magazine, inviting passengers to e-mail her directly about their experiences with her airline. She ensures that everyone who does receives a reply! Within 2 years of starting to use the Web for bookings, the vast majority of ticket sales for these airlines were carried out online, saving huge amounts of staff costs and delivering a much better service to their customers.

- The international hotel group, Marriott, allows its customers to check out its rates and availability of rooms online in real time, and then allows them to book, thereby reducing the use of its call centres (and, incidentally, allowing a better service to be given to customers who prefer to call). Not only can it save transaction costs, but Marriott found that it increased room occupancy by allowing customers to book rooms at the last minute.

- The National Express coach division increased its direct sales by 29 per cent within 6 months of implementing a CRM strategy. One of the methods they used was to target students on their database during November (traditionally a quiet month), with offers of trips to anywhere in the country for £10.

- Courier services such as FedEx, DSL and TNT allow customers to dial straight into their database, to track exactly where their packages are during transit. The customers get better service because it is quick and easy to use, while the couriers save enormously on call centre costs.

Easier said than done . . .

While the concepts behind CRM are relatively simple to grasp, putting theory into practice is another thing altogether. Many companies have great difficulty in identifying their customers in the first place. Even if they can, identifying who are the most profitable now and who are likely to become the most profitable in the future is not an easy task.

Many businesses fail to grasp what their customers actually want, from which products they are likely to buy to the level of service they require. And many more have never really worked out whether the customer-centric practices in their business model actually achieve the customer retention goals sought in the first place. Indeed, these practices need to be perpetually refined if they are to work, because people move on and competitors can easily be ahead of the game in delivering customer satisfaction.

As we will see on Thursday, implementing CRM within your business has to be a company-wide commitment. The implications for any organisation to adopt CRM are huge, but the process has to be evolutionary rather than an overnight sensation. Piecemeal CRM is not an option. A customer-centric organisation must have its culture emanate from the board and it must be at the very heart of the business.

Summary

CRM is becoming increasingly important for all organisations looking to provide better service to their customers at substantially lower costs.

The most important thing to remember is that all that data collection, all that updating and all that profiling is based on the objective of building a relationship with the customer.

The further the customer gets away from the people within the company, the less likelihood there is of the customer feeling that there is any kind of relationship. All human values depend on the relationships that are built and CRM, of its very essence, is the building of a virtual relationship with the customer, which we, as business people can manage to our advantage as well as to that of the customer.

For customers to value a relationship with a company, it either has to deliver something of value to them or deliver something that has a perceived value. So if the potential data collection is thought through from this basic viewpoint then your data capture will be useful and not become tangential.

Because of long term neglect of customer wants and needs, CRM has become a burning issue, but its need to become systemic throughout an organisation is often difficult to bring to reality. Anticipating customer demands and ensuring that customer expectations are not higher than those you can deliver is a fine art and requires the diligence and devotion that any relationship deserves.

Although CRM is often enabled by technology, it has to be viewed as a concept that stems from and to every aspect of the business. It encompasses everything to do with a customer relationship and its sole *raison d'être* is to make the customers not only feel valued, but to know that they are valued and that their wants are being fulfilled and aspirations met.

Companies will only achieve this by integrating customer data, keeping it updated, and using it to anticipate demand for their products and services, while delivering customer satisfaction.

The customer

You may remember the days when most major retailers and service companies had 'complaints departments'. You may also remember – not so long ago – when the word 'service' appeared to be a concept totally alien to some shop assistants and maintenance engineers. Who was it that said business would be so much easier without customers to worry about?

People in the UK and the rest of Europe laughed when the expression *'Have a nice day!'* started being used everywhere across the pond. Surely no one could really be stupid enough to believe that an overused, well-worn expression could impact on what the customer actually thought about the company offering its products and services? However, perhaps it made a positive and proactive impression on the employee who uttered the magic words.

If the British have learned anything from their American counterparts, it is that a company that values its customers and goes out of its way to make them feel good, has a much

better chance of succeeding than a company that does not seem to care what the customer thinks.

Why should this be?

It is obvious that if you get a bad deal from a firm, you are going to think twice before using their goods or services again. That has always been the case. So why should the rules of the corporate game have changed so much since those days when service was a dirty word and regarded as almost unnecessary?

There are basically four reasons why customers of today are more tyrannical than they ever used to be.

Rapidly increasing productivity has led, in many areas, to overcapacity. This, in turn, makes each customer more important; the customers are no longer king, they have become dictators! The buyers have much more information at their fingertips and many more options for the products and services they want to buy.

Comparing prices of similar offerings to see which gives better value for money is now easy. It is no longer necessary to put up with 'inflated' prices, because it is much easier to find goods elsewhere.

The quality of goods and services is being driven higher all the time by improved technology. In fact, it is becoming increasingly difficult to differentiate between offerings (consider automotive sales, or financial services, for instance). The result is that competing products are becoming more alike every day. If you cannot compete on the product offering itself or on the cost, then something else is bound to play a major part in sales.

The pace of life is getting faster and, in general, customers are more stressed than they ever used to be. Given the power customers have attained due to the previous three scenarios, they are unlikely to be in the mood to accept shoddy goods, poor service or even slow delivery. When there was no choice but to buy telephone services from British Telecom, gas from British Gas and our banking services from one of the 'Big Four' high street banks, people had nowhere else to go. Now that has all changed. We no longer have to put up with bad service. Customers can take their business elsewhere – and without leaving their houses or offices to visit company premises as previously!

So, with falling profit margins, better access to competitors' information, better quality and more demanding customers, the only thing for a company to do is either invent a new state-of-the-art 'me too' product, and/or to compete in the way that it treats its customers.

Valuing your customers

In terms of the cost of sales, it is an old truism that it is more expensive to attract a new customer than to retain an old one. The travel company, Thomas Cook, puts the ratio at 5:1 – i.e. winning new customers is five times more expensive than keeping existing ones.

If you think of the amount that most companies spend on advertising, the vast majority of that – probably over 75 per cent of it – is spent on attracting new customers. After all, a 'captured' customer already happy with the goods or services offered by a company does not have to be persuaded of the company's merits. They are known already and have become a given factor.

It follows that the longer a business keeps a customer, the more profitable the customer is for the company. And the longer the customer stays loyal, the more the relationship is reinforced and it is less likely that the customer will be wooed by other companies' offerings. Equally important, the more loyal your customers become, the more likely they will be to promote you, your brand, products and services to friends and acquaintances.

What motivates a customer?

Sadly, some of the larger institutions, such as the high street banks, have learned to their cost that offering preferential deals to new customers ('free' banking for a year, for instance) and expecting long-term customers to accept second-class treatment is an almost guaranteed way of driving long-term clients into the arms of competitors. The almost overnight success of recent institutions such as Egg, Smile.com and IF are good examples, if proof were needed. These companies offered amazing deals to attract customers in the first place and to take a significant market share from a standing start. It will be interesting to see whether they can keep that market share when they are perceived as more 'normal'.

To improve the bottom line in any business, an analysis of what motivates a person to become a customer is paramount.

Understanding your potential clients and building a relationship with them is the only way to motivate them to part with their hard-earned cash.

Therefore, it is instructive to understand what motivation is all about. Potential customers can be motivated for a number of different reasons – some overt and some hidden in the subconscious. Take the everyday act of shopping, for instance. Why do we do it?

- Necessity for the product or service
- It makes a change from routine
- There is great stimulation in looking for (and finding) a bargain
- Pressure from peer groups
- The sheer enjoyment of spending money

There are plenty of other reasons too, of course. In the main, these are all obvious. However, what makes a person choose one manufacturer's product or service over another? Often the reasons include a subconscious decision on the part of the customer. But some important questions need to be asked:

- How necessary is the product – essential or optional?
- Is the product/service seen as a pleasure or a task?
- What is the perceived cost?
- What are the perceived risks?
- Are there lots of other competitive products on the market?
- Does it have a 'me too' factor?

Not for nothing are insurance salespeople taught that the two main motivators for clinching a sale are fear and greed!

If an organisation can appreciate what motivates a potential customer (whether it is an individual or business customer), only then can it begin to predict, and then change, customer behaviour. Think about the buying sequence, for example. Almost every transaction is based on the following pattern:

- The customer thinks about their needs or desires
- They assess available marketing material and back this up by asking for, and (sometimes) receiving, advice
- They think about alternative ways of satisfying their needs
- They assess whether the benefits are in line with the costs
- Once they have made their purchase they weigh up whether the product or service was as expected

The experience of this purchase will impact upon any future purchasing decisions in this particular product or service area.

Segmenting your customers

As we have already seen, people buy products for different reasons. A company that concentrates on one aspect of consumer decision making will inevitably lose valuable sales.

Consumers, whether end-user or business-to-business customers, can be categorised in a number of ways. Various mathematical models have been built to predict consumer behaviour.

For instance, you could split them into four camps:

1 *Passive consumer*: easily swayed by marketing promotions, an impulsive buyer who does not necessarily use logic in buying decisions.
2 *Emotional consumer*: depending on their moods or emotions, will often purchase on a whim, for instant gratification or to have something 'new' to show they are up to speed.
3 *Economic consumer*: often goes to extraordinary lengths to analyse all the information about a product before parting with their money.
4 *Cognitive consumer*: somewhat risk-averse, will make hard and fast decisions based on time spent, economics, physiological needs and psychological reasons.

In a business-to-business relationship, economic and cognitive consumers dominate purchasing by necessity.

How does your local supermarket lay out its offerings? Most of them, regardless of which chain they belong to, follow a set plan. Magazines are often placed at the front of the store to attract the impulse buyer who probably had not thought about buying that particular journal on the way to the store; chocolates and other confectionery are placed near the check-out tills for those who want instant satisfaction on leaving the shop. By giving the price per litre or kilogram that a unit sells for, in addition to its overall price, the store caters for the analysts amongst its customers, quite apart from adhering to the law. Special price discounts in most departments even encourage the risk-averse to part with their cash in a not entirely planned way.

These four categories of consumers are, by their very nature, crude breakdowns. They can all be broken down further using other factors such as, culture, education, social environment, nationality, demographics and so on. Business customers can also be further analysed depending on their buying cycle, budgets and pressing current needs, for example.

Simply put, market segmentation is defined as the subdivision of a market into homogenous subsets; each of these subsets can be regarded as a target market in its own right and reached with a distinctive marketing mix. These subsets need to be treated in slightly different ways when managing the customer relationships.

By analysing its customer base, an organisation can discover significant differences as well as similarities in their clients. If the differences and similarities are segmented, it should be possible to predict the motivating factors behind the different groups of customers, thereby offering them a more personalised service to 'help' them make a buying decision more easily.

Take Amazon.co.uk, for instance. This world-famous internet bookstore tries to predict the type of books that its customers might be interested in. The more you, the potential customer, delve into its database of books, the more information Amazon receives what type of books you are interested in and which authors you might like to read about. But it goes much further than this. Amazon knows that you have bought a book on CRM by Langford-Wood and Salter, and it can see what other consumers who have bought the book order next. This may be other books in the *In a week* series; other books by Langford-Wood and Salter; other CRM-related titles or indeed, all three. Using this information, Amazon suggests other books that you might be interested in. Of course, you may choose to ignore their recommendations, but because the plug for another book is based on data from other consumers in your segmentation category, it is likely to close another sale.

Until quite recently, collecting and sorting this kind of data was a mammoth task beyond the capabilities of most organisations. However, the newer technologies have made it possible and organisations can gather and manage the data in real time. We shall look at this further on Tuesday.

What is the best way to break a market down into segments? As we have said, there are many ways to split up a market, but ideally you need to ask yourself some basic questions:

- Can you clearly differentiate this segment from other market segments?
- Will all members of the segment react in a uniform way to your marketing messages?
- Is the segment big enough to warrant the extra expense incurred in catering for it?
- Will the customers within this segment recognise themselves, or will they instead reject their enforced categorisation?
- Can you access the particular segment easily or is it beyond the reach of your delivery channels?
- Will this segment offer above average returns and make it worthwhile segmenting in the first place?

Organisations can also use predictive techniques to identify customers who might defect to a competitor. By analysing small groups of like-minded customers, it can spot signs of discontent shown by decreasing activity within the group and by other signs of potential defection. If a group suffers a defection, others in that same group might act in a similar way; the early warning signs are there for the organisation to discover and to do something about before the entire segment drifts away.

A word of warning! Many organisations segment their prospects by how people have reacted in a given situation, or through an analysis of past sales. Unfortunately, the past does not guarantee the future; the world as we know it is changing so quickly that you can no longer simply extrapolate the past and expect it to apply to the future.

This does not mean that we should ignore the past. There are always valuable lessons to be learned, which should guide us away from some of the elephant traps lying on the road to future prosperity. Nevertheless, we should use the insight gained from the past to help us think laterally and holistically for the future, knowing that our predictions are almost certain to be wrong, but equally that they should help us to reduce our margin of error.

Summary

It is a sad fact of life that competition for customers has never been hotter between organisations wishing to sell their products and services.

Customers are much more demanding than they ever were and, since differentiation of products and services is becoming harder, potential customers are more likely to base their buying decisions upon levels of service and personalisation of service, than on product differentiation.

Existing customers are more valuable to an organisation than new ones because the cost of sale is necessarily lower and the profit margin per retained customer is so much higher.

It is essential for a company to stop and analyse what motivates their customers, and to understand that although some motivation is overt, there are numerous undercurrents of subconscious motivators that affect everybody's buying decisions. For instance, if you go to a garage to buy a new car, the salesperson will be keen to tell you that the cars have 'alloy wheels' even though most people are not really interested in this feature. Car salespeople believe they are important; the motor trade thinks they are important, but the majority of customers do not. So why do the salespeople still plug alloy wheels on the cars they are selling?

Organisations can significantly improve the effectiveness of their marketing activity by segmenting customers and prospective customers into easily identifiable groups. This will lead to a better penetration of those markets and generate better profits. After all, most organisations cannot afford to deal with individual customers, but they can deal with segments and still get a personalised message across to individuals.

Segmentation will help you to understand the needs of your customers in order for you to develop your relationships with them. You will be able to allocate limited marketing resources among the potentially most profitable segments and the customers will feel that you understand them and that they have a relationship with your firm; they will want to do business with you.

Customers are only people, and people respond to flattery, good service and being made to feel wanted. As part of the personalisation that good CRM brings, the organisation needs to make its customers feel like individuals. This can only be done if customers stop being thought of as just another consumer and, instead, are made to feel like individual clients of a company that knows and values them.

Channels

Having made the decision to become more acquainted with its customers, an organisation must begin by creating a comprehensive customer database. Each customer needs to be given a unique database identity because overtly personalised services and one-to-one activities will form the basis for any enduring relationship.

Note that we are not talking about holding a simple database of customer account details such as address, phone number, account number, how much they owe, and so on. The point of this database is not simply to generate additional marketing activities to be targeted at the customer. First, the company needs to use the database to build relationships and loyalty and then – and only then – should marketing be targeted at the customer. Attempting to flood the customer with marketing materials before attempting to find out what they want can be totally counter-productive, and could even succeed in turning them off the brand.

The reason for creating a personalised service should be to ensure that any offerings from the company fit the customers' profiles so well that, in theory, they should never want to go elsewhere for their particular products or services. A well-honed personalised service will result in customer loyalty and, therefore, greater demand for additional products or services.

Once a relationship is built, the more ways in which a customer is given to interact with the company, the stronger the relationship is likely to be. The customer can then contact and interact with you as a business in whatever way suits them best – any time, by any means and from anywhere.

For instance, say you were a long-term customer of a bank, but that you moved house to a village where there was only a competing bank's branch. It might not be convenient for you to travel all the way to the nearest town to continue your banking, and you might, therefore, be tempted to move your account to the competition. However, you may be very happy to use the internet for your banking transactions, in which case you could access your existing bank's online offering from your new home, and not feel the need to have a physical bank in your vicinity.

On the other hand, having decided to make the switch from 'terrestrial' banking to online banking, you might find that the offerings from the traditional high street banks, bore little or no comparison to the vastly superior interest rates and online facilities offered by the likes of Smile, Egg and IF – but how long for? Product curves go down as well as up, and so will the interest rates if the rest of the pack catch up and leap-frog over the new kids on the block.

The fact is that, in today's world, customers no longer need to tolerate being dictated to. As a result, many organisations supplement their traditional bricks-and-mortar network with direct sales forces and telephone facilities that are open up to 24 hours a day. Companies have rushed to take advantage of an online presence, but the internet is only one channel reaching an increasingly demanding and potentially fickle clientele.

The more channels a business offers a customer, the more likely the customer is to be loyal. There are many channels that can reach a prospect, as well as an existing client, but when an organisation becomes truly multi-channel in its approach, it is possible to offer the highest levels of service at the lowest possible overhead because of the convenience offered to the customers. If you have reached that happy state of nirvana, think about how new competitors are going to poach your existing customers away.

Putting theory into practice

Unfortunately, few organisations have attained a zenith in their corporate horizons. Some are so in need of revenue that they oversell their products before offering a truly personalised level of service. Some will diversify into so many different areas that they are unable to reinforce their communities of customers. Some build websites that are totally sales oriented, rather than service oriented, and the resulting messages to the customer become confused and fragmented.

Companies that offer numerous customer interfaces must ensure that whichever channel the customer uses to interact with the company, they receive the same level of service. Just because customers use different channels to reach you, does not mean they will be happy if they cannot view you as one company. That means that the response they receive from your call centre should be on a par with their experience of, say, visiting your website.

Perceptions of a company

Different perceptions in different countries also give very different views of the same company. For instance, in the spring of 2002, Amazon.co.uk topped the loyalty list in Europe. German retail websites had the greatest number of loyal customers in Europe, while Italy and Switzerland had the least. However, brand loyalty to Amazon differed markedly across the continent, with Switzerland having the lowest retention rate with only 28 per cent of November's customers coming back 3 months later. By comparison, 40 per cent of the company's visitors were returning to the site 3 months later in the UK.

In France, CDiscount.com led the retail category, retaining 53 per cent of its customers, while Rueducommerce.fr ranked a close second with a 52 per cent retention rate.

In the UK, Tesco.com had a high level of loyalty, with more than one-third of unique visitors going back to the site 3 months later. However, brands that perform well on the high street – Argos, Comet and John Lewis – only managed to retain between 12 per cent and 16 per cent of their November website visitors.

Reducing costs

Moreover, the fact that your company communicates with customers, does not mean that it is offering them any benefits. Ideally, you want the customer to interact seamlessly with both your company's systems and staff, rather than only with members of your staff, since costs rise dramatically the more staff involved.

On the other hand, service levels can rise dramatically with the degree of interactivity offered by a channel. We say *can* because there are plenty of instances where customers can interact with your systems and feel thoroughly frustrated by the experience. For instance, think of the times you have attempted to call a company, only to be forced to go through endless iterations of '*If you are an existing customer, press 1; or a new customer press 2*' and so on.

In a multi-channel environment some channels are, by their very nature, more dependent on human intervention than others. For instance, all of these channels need human intervention:

* Correspondence via the postal service (snail mail)
* Fax
* E-mail
* Bricks and mortar, face-to-face meetings
* Call centres

While the following can be completely automated:

- Website offerings
- Mobile phone text messaging
- EDI (Electronic Data) systems
- ATM (Automatic Teller Machine, hole-in-the-wall cash machines)
- Touch-screen kiosk
- Interactive voice response unit
- Satellite TV set-top box offering interactive services

Those same channel categories can be sorted in a different way – interactive and non-interactive:

Non-interactive:

- Correspondence via the postal service (snail mail)
- Fax
- E-mail
- Website offerings (information sites)
- Mobile phone text messaging
- EDI (Electronic Data) systems

Interactive:

- Bricks and mortar, face-to-face meetings
- Website offerings (processing sites)
- Call Centres
- ATM (hole-in-the-wall cash machines)
- Touch-screen kiosk
- Interactive voice response unit
- Satellite TV set-top box offering interactive services

The more you can automate your customer contacts, the lower your operational costs, and the more interactivity you can offer, the better satisfied your client base. From this it becomes clear that non-human interactive channels offer the best levels of service for the lowest operational cost.

Thus, the best service, per cost, channels are offered by:

- Website offerings (processing sites)
- ATM (hole-in-the-wall cash machines)
- Touch-screen kiosk
- Interactive voice response unit
- Satellite TV set-top box offering interactive services

On the other hand, some companies get so totally taken over by the software to enable non-people interfaces, they lose some of the personalised areas that could prove to be more cost-effective. For example, does your research convince you that an automated telephone menu system is actually the best for you and most cost effective? Or have you considered whether it might be as quick, and cost much the same, to have real people answering the telephone and putting customers through to the correct department for their queries?

The cost of annoying some customers by leaving them to press button responses may outweigh the cost of letting them talk to a person straightaway.

As you can see, although the internet has had a huge impact on the way businesses run and on the means by which they can interact with their client base, it is by no means the only technological way of interaction, nor necessarily the best.

Take e-mail, for instance. Incoming electronic mail is not really geared up to providing quality customer service. To start with, it will not offer immediate information to customers who have come to expect information to be available when they want it. In fact, they are more likely to reach for the phone. The cost of processing incoming e-mails is similar to dealing with post, overall making it an expensive mechanism to deliver poor service.

It makes more sense to encourage users to find the information they want from a website. They can enter their search criteria into a search engine and be almost instantaneously offered the facts they want. Further, if the website can first identify who they are and discover if they already have a profile in the company database, it can deliver content specifically geared to that one individual.

Outbound e-mail is a different kettle of fish. Generating personalised e-mails from information held within a company database, with hyperlinks to information that the customer might find useful, can achieve a high level of service for very little unit cost.

For instance, an order could be acknowledged by e-mail that contains a link to an order tracking Web page and this could offer further options such as delivery terms or packaging requirements.

Auto-response technologies have been one of the fastest growth areas in available CRM systems. Modern systems can search for keywords in e-mails and suggest a number of responses, rated according to their probable relevancy to the client. In some systems, a proposed answer is routed through a human interface to check that the response is appropriate, and it is then forwarded on to the client. However, more and more companies are moving to the completely automated response.

Research shows that a well coordinated approach to using multiple channels can reduce selling costs by over 20 per cent. This can be achieved, for example, by using low-cost systems to develop and qualify sales leads, and then switching to higher cost, but closer contact channels (such as the direct sales force) to close the sale.

There are other benefits than lowering costs. In most markets, any one channel will normally only account for 50 per cent of the potential market volume, if that. To 'capture' the market, an organisation needs to offer other channels to customers, to avoid losing out to the competition.

There is another advantage. In some cases, offering multiple channels can produce what is known as 'channel synergy'. To put it another way, the effect of channels working together can be greater than the sum of the benefits offered by the individual parts. An example of this is ordering tickets from many of the low cost airlines. Customers are encouraged to order over the Web but can always ring directly as well.

Customers do have preferences

Although most customers will use multiple channels to interact with a supply company, they do tend to use them in predictable or set ways. A company that can identify these preferences can save a great deal of its costs.

For instance, when you go to the bank, do you do so just to pay in money, or to withdraw money as well? Do you prefer to use an ATM machine to withdraw money? Do you ever use an ATM to make deposits? Does your bank enable you to make deposits using their ATMs? Those who do not have a gap in the customer service loop.

Some banks and building societies encourage their customers to use an ATM or the internet rather than a service desk, because it is obviously cheaper for them not to pay for additional staff. Typically, an ATM transaction will cost the bank one-quarter of the cost of a personal contact, while an internet transaction might only cost 1 per cent of the assistant's costs. Accordingly, the interest rates offered tend to be higher for card-only or internet-only accounts; customers are discovering they have to pay more for a personal service if they want one.

Internet service providers have also discovered that it makes economic sense – and is more user-friendly to customers – to post service information (i.e. how to configure a particular e-mail client or Web browser) onto a website. They also discourage users, usually through making a charge, from ringing their call centre operators.

Organisations are also finding that individuals respond in very different ways, depending on the channel used to convey information.

For example, neither of us like being 'cold called' by telemarketing sales agents, whatever it is they may be selling. They are invariably reading from a script and are working on a commission basis. They often give the impression that they are not interested in what we want, but in what they can earn for themselves. It does not help that often the scripts are ill-prepared and the training of the agent appears minimal. This may be as a result of telesales centres believing their own hype about being able to sell anything. Or perhaps it is a reflection of companies running on a tight budget. Nevertheless, this backfires because the target customers

know that a company which has not equipped its staff with the correct knowledge, is unlikely to care about its customers but is simply after a quick profit.

On the other hand, the inbox of our e-mail account is often full of 'special offers' that allow us to fly off to the sun for less than £10, or to pick up a bargain at some online store. Although we have been targeted as part of a wider consumer group, we can block such advertising if we want to or jet off to distant climates if the fancy takes us.

Same product, different channel.

Synchronising channels

Whichever channel customers use to interact with an organisation, be it e-mail, letter, telephone, fax or in person, these interactions should be tracked and recorded in order to maintain a seamless dialogue between the client and the company.

If, for instance, one of your customers sends an e-mail complaint and follows this up with a phone call the next day, the company should be aware of the complaint e-mail. Unfortunately, few companies have managed to synchronise systems to this extent.

In time, organisations should aim to go even further. In a fully integrated system, every enquiry that comes in – whether by e-mail, letter, fax or phone – should be routed through a procedure that can gauge its urgency, identify whether it is a complaint or a request for information and, most importantly, determine the 'valuable' or 'low-valve' status of the customer.

If the customer database recognises that one missive is from a frequent long-term buyer, it makes sense to give this high priority and even to route it to a sales agent to deal with immediately. Instead of the customer having to make a follow up call, the agent can call the customer and, hopefully, deal with the problem there and then.

The customer will feel better about the company and the company may have saved the customer from the clutches of the competition.

Summary

By utilising technology and offering customers multiple ways of interacting with it, an organisation can significantly improve the customer experience and strengthen customer loyalty.

As technologies develop and costs invariably fall further, a fully-integrated customer relationship system will become attractive to most businesses. The customer will be able to interact with a company seamlessly, be it in person, by e-mail, via the internet, by phone, or through any chosen channel.

By ensuring customer satisfaction – and delight – companies will be able to bring together business processes, partners and channels in order to win new customers and strengthen bonds with existing clients.

Call centres and help desks

We were recently called upon to go to Helsinki to give a speech to an organisation called Yhteys – the Finnish Help-Desk Association.

In discussions after the speech, we told them of our experiences with an internationally known British company who we regularly have to phone in order to get anything remotely resembling a service. The company did not offer an e-mail or internet service at the time.

We told the Finns that whenever we called the organisation we were usually routed through numerous interactive voice response units and had music played at us for an average of 29 minutes, before we got to speak to anybody at all. Furthermore, there was no other way of getting the questions answered.

The reaction from the audience in Helsinki indicated that this was the biggest joke they had heard during the 3-day conference. We were told in response, that if they did not

answer the phone within four rings they were liable to lose their jobs!

Customers that want everything

Customers, as we have already seen, have become tyrants. On the one hand they are looking for improved quality; on the other hand they want to pay less for it. They want organisations to be more flexible; but they also want faster responses and truthful answers.

Of these four conflicting desires, possibly the most critical factor in winning a customer over is the response time of a company. If we have a complaint, we are all impressed with a company if it calls back, appears genuinely concerned and responsive, and – better still – responds quickly to our original complaint.

One of our clients wished to transfer their internet account from an ISP that had given poor dial-up access for some time. They decided to move across to Clara.net for their internet services. Unfortunately, due to an error that we discovered later had nothing to do with Clara, our client was unable to access the premium service for which they had already paid.

What a pleasure it was to find that Clara regularly rang us to apologise for the mix up and to tell us what was going on. A specific named individual 'took possession' of the problem and when it was finally sorted out, offered compensation to say sorry for something one of their suppliers had done incorrectly. What a refreshing change, we felt.

Or is it?

More and more companies have discovered that call centres,
help desks (call them what you will) have to be perceived as
positively responsive to customer enquiries, to make them
stand out from the competition. The technology behind call
centres is relatively simple, but getting the right mix between
the economics of offering the facility and the demands of
customers is something that many organisations are still
learning.

In general, call centres represent the public face of an
organisation, and the resulting level of customer satisfaction
is directly proportional to the quality of the processes
involved and the empathy of the people staffing the centre.

We have already seen that the benefits of a properly run call
centre are:

- To provide a quick and easy way for customers and
  prospective customers to have their questions
  answered
- To be a single point of contact for gathering
  customer information and feedback
- To offer a controlled process for the consistent
  treatment of customers, regardless of which channel
  they use when approaching the company
- To offer customers increased satisfaction through
  increased convenience
- To improve productivity among sales staff by
  qualifying leads and offering other support

To assist call centres trying to achieve customer nirvana, a huge assortment of help-desk tools has been developed. These range from simple call-logging software on a stand-alone PC to fully integrated customer support systems which interact with back-end company databases and knowledge repositories.

However large or small the system, they all have common characteristics in the way they handle calls, namely:

- Logging
- Allocation
- Resolution
- Tracking

Call logging
The first point of contact with a help desk is crucial both in the way the customer views the company and in the way the company handles the call. Some systems can identify what equipment the caller is using; most have pop-up screens which help the operator classify the call, assessing the magnitude of the problem or query, and prioritising the call. Caller line identification allows the back-end system to bring up the likely details of each customer before a single word is actually spoken (provided that the phone line has been used by the caller before). By simply keying in a caller's postcode, more details regarding the customer can appear instantaneously on screen.

Call allocation
Many help desks attempt to solve the problem of allocation

directly, with the operator taking the call. Others allocate the call to back-end staff, more familiar with the problem or query. In fact, there is nothing more irritating for customers than to find that the operators they are talking to have even less idea about their problems than they have. When the operator reads from a prepared script, it can often have the opposite effect from that intended and really annoy the customer.

By allocating the call to specialists, however, some advanced systems are capable of identifying available skills or real-time availability of specialist engineers. Call centres run by the AA and RAC are typical examples of this type of arrangement. Providing links to the pagers or e-mail systems of these travelling experts means that the call centre can arrange the fastest turn around from receiving the call to getting someone out to help.

Call resolution
More advanced systems can store details about the various services that can be offered to a customer. In this way, problems that cannot be resolved at initial contact can be escalated to more senior or specialist staff.

These same systems can retrieve information gleaned from previous calls on the same subject; earlier retained knowledge is often a good route to finding if the same problem is recurring. Similarly, monitoring and diagnostic tools can allow the operator to run through all obvious and specific checks, with a set pattern or route map to follow depending on the answer to each question. This type of call centre is very common in computer suppliers' help desks because many of the problems that customers have are predictable and often repeated, much the same as the Frequently Asked Questions (FAQs) which are included on most websites.

Once a problem has been resolved, the call data is stored for future analysis of the call management system – how much has been achieved during the time spent on it – and adds to the store of knowledge of potential customers' problems and queries.

Call tracking
Any half-decent system should be able to monitor a call throughout its entire progress, through the various operators who are dealing with it. The system should be able to give instant statistics to management on the status of traffic coming in to the call centre. Most call centres have displays showing the number of calls waiting to be answered, the average length of time taken to deal with a call and even the 'productivity' of each operator calculated by the amount of calls he or she has been able to handle.

One well-known company has a rule that each of its operators should spend no more than 40 seconds on any incoming call before passing it on to someone else down the chain or dealing with it completely. The frustration this causes for the hapless customers is immense. The impression is routinely given that the operator does not care about the callers' problems, the staff themselves sound demoralised, and no one wins – except perhaps for the call centre managers who can rightly claim that they have instituted a system for passing through callers in a timely manner.

SORRY, SIR, YOUR 40 SECONDS ARE UP.
I'LL HAVE TO PASS YOU ON TO THE NEXT
OPERATOR.

So, why did the company set up a call centre in the first place if not to meet the needs of its customers? The answer, you may have gathered, probably lies in the fact that it is a privatised utility that used to have a captive market and the company is only now coming to grips with the fact that there is real competition out there. They realise that they need to shake up their ideas to avoid losing their entire market share in the future!

The benefits of a call management system are easy to see:

- They can offer a fast speed of response
- Customers can feel they are getting individual attention
- Customers can get help when they need it at a time that suits them
- Handled correctly, the company can offer a professional service to customers
- A complete audit trail can be recorded for each call

- Problems can be identified early on in the lifecycle of a product
- By allowing general operators to filter calls, specialist staff can spend their time more productively dealing with the more difficult problems
- Reduced costs in supporting customers
- Increased customer satisfaction

Nonetheless, it is vital to remember, as we shall see on Thursday, that however good your system may be, it simply will not work if the underlying business process is a mess. Similarly, if a central call centre is passing queries on to a number of more specialist call centres, each of the centres has to work seamlessly with one another; the entire system is only as robust as the weakest unit.

Advanced technology

The pace of technological progress is such that anything written about advanced technology is likely to appear very dated in a short space of time. However, the principles behind some of the technologies do not change; it is only in their implementation that speed and accuracy can improve.

For instance, take the automated call distributor (ACD). In the early 1990s, the ACD was only found in the most advanced centres. The ACD routes calls evenly around the operators and shortens queuing time to a minimum. Now it is ubiquitous and management can have a clear view of which operators are handling the most calls, the average waiting time for a customer, the average time it takes an operator to close a call and much more besides.

Many call centres (for example, London Transport's enquiry unit) have displays prominently featured on their walls for all the operators to see, at a glance, the status of their network. It is claimed that this acts as a powerful motivator for the operators.

Most call centres have now introduced interactive voice response units. Callers are asked to key in a number on their telephones in response to a menu of offerings. Newer systems can process voice responses where the caller is asked to say 'yes' or 'no' in response to each option.

This was thought to be an excellent idea when first introduced, because in theory the caller can get to the right type of person in the shortest possible time. However, there has been quite a backlash from customers about this impersonal way of being dealt with at the first point of contact with the company and many organisations have returned to a manual operator who carries out the first sifting of the callers. Automated systems and delays can be equally annoying to customers and both can be counter-productive for customer satisfaction. If they are not implemented with a customer-centric mind-set and do not have enough real operators to answer queries not readily dealt with in an automated manner they can prove problematic.

Knowledge base

When customers or potential customers ring a call centre, they do so normally for one of three reasons:

1 They are looking for information
2 They wish to make a complaint
3 They wish to place an order

To service these calls, the system needs to be able to:

1 Find specific information from a vast repository stored on different media
2 Enable several operators to work together, pooling data from the system
3 Help front-line operators to handle a call without passing on the call to specialists, unless absolutely necessary

At the simplest level, flow charts can be prepared by specialists, advising what do to in a given set of circumstances: *'If so-and-so happens then follow route A, otherwise follow route B'*.

By using intranet technology and entering key words into a search engine, staff can search for answers using a hypertext system that jumps straight to the relevant data they need. This type of system can also handle frequently asked questions (FAQs), where experts initially compile a library of precedents for lay operators to deal knowledgeably with a particular problem.

The benefits of using such systems are indisputable.

- Staff do not have to 'reinvent the wheel' every time someone else calls with a similar problem
- More problems can be solved at the first point of contact, rather than having to pass customers on to more expensive 'experts'
- The answers given out by a company are consistent – adding credibility to a company's offerings
- Call durations are minimised
- Operators need less training time

Contact centres

Call centres have long proved their worth to companies. However, with the advent of internet technologies, many companies are now transforming their call centres into contact centres, dealing with customers over the Web as well as using traditional phone calls.

In these new centres, the same operators that deal with phone calls also handle e-mails. Unfortunately, this is still causing tremendous problems because people are still getting to grips with prioritising incoming queries.

The problem stems from the fact that people who send an e-mail expect a fast response, even if the query itself is not viewed by the company as being a priority call. In much the same way, a fax is often regarded by the sender as 'more urgent' than a letter. It is interesting to note that a telephone call will still be answered during most person-to-person meetings, as a priority over continuing the meeting. It is as if

the old metaphor, 'a bird in the hand is worth two in the bush', can be taken to new extremes. The receiver of the telephone call is assuming that the person in their meeting is already 'theirs' and that by answering the phone they have a chance to get one of the two customers in the bush as well!

Priority in any case is often given to phone-based work because it is all too easy to think that someone on the end of a line is more impatient for an answer than someone who has fired off an e-mail. Think what happens when you are having a discussion with someone and the phone rings. Do you answer the phone and leave your colleague waiting, or do you leave the phone to ring and finish your conversation first?

Technology also allows automated e-mail responses that acknowledge receipt of the e-mail and ensure that an operator will deal with it as soon as possible. This causes its own problems: it raises expectations that a fast response is forthcoming, but the centres may then find they cannot service the query until much later in the day.

This has a knock-on effect and customers who have not received a reply may send a second e-mail or even phone the call centre, increasing the pressure on the operators and obviating the benefits that an e-mail presence was designed to offer. Due to this, many centres look for a maximum turn around time for e-mails of 4 hours, although there are still many contact centre managers who believe that a 24-hour turn around, or longer, is good enough.

Problems are exacerbated further when you consider that a routine phone call to a contact centre takes on average from 30 seconds to 1 minute, whereas online contacts take on average between 2 to 4 minutes each to deal with – a four-fold increase in time taken.

Another point to bear in mind is that telephone traffic tends to be busiest in the morning and late afternoon, while internet enquiries tend to be quiet during the day and peak between 8 p.m. and midnight. This means that the introduction of Web-based responses will, of necessity, mean revamping the staff rota to cope with the evening traffic.

Summary

Organisations have discovered that call centres, help desks and contact centres have to be seen to be responsive to customer enquiries, to make them stand out from the competition and not be dismissed as 'One of those awful call centres where they don't know who you are, keep you waiting and can't answer the question anyway'. If your firm gets complaints like this, you have to assume that there is a lot of work and analysis needed on your customer relationship management system.

A centre needs to have in place the means to log calls and allocate them to the correct person to deal with. More advanced systems can glean information from each call and add this to a knowledge base accessed by both front-line operators and management. Ideally, it will also track individual calls and give meaningful statistics to management, in order to run the centre more efficiently.

The knowledge acquired from the call centre is invaluable in honing customer-centric future products and services, in identifying problems with existing offerings and in tailoring an efficient and user-friendly company–customer. Delivering customer satisfaction is the aim.

Company culture and attitude

A personal example

We recently decided in our office to get some new cars. We had no difficulty in finding a dealer who was able to offer a superb range of second-hand cars each with very low mileage.

We rang them to find an extremely helpful and knowledgeable lady who answered our questions promptly, promised to come back to us with more information following our questions, e-mailed the information to us within 12 hours, and then telephoned us to see if there was anything else we needed to know. Our first impressions were excellent and, having decided which model of car we wanted, we had no hesitation in placing our order through this dealership.

A few days later, the cars we had ordered were ready and we set off on the 40-mile journey to go to collect them. On the drivers' seats were a bunch of flowers and a bottle of red wine.

We drove back to the office feeling very pleased with the service we had received.

The same day, however, we discovered that the drawer under the seat in one of the cars was sticking badly and was difficult to open. We rang the dealership to ask what we should do. *'Stay where you are'*, came the reply; and within an hour, the managing director was on our doorstep with a tool-kit and a replacement.

Two days later the petrol filler cap on the other car refused to open. Ringing the nearest manufacturer service centre, we were told that a new part would need to be fitted but that it was an easy job to do and could be done in 5 minutes if we took it over to them.

Before we did so we rang the dealership, mentioning this problem. *'Stay where you are'*, came the reply once again; and the managing director once again made the 80-mile round trip to our office, this time on a wet and blustery evening to fit another lock. Although the car was second-hand, and there was no way the dealership could have known that the lock unit would fail, they took full responsibility for the problem and put things right immediately.

As the dealership explained to us, it is the personal relationship between organisations and their customers that makes or breaks a deal, and they have put customer satisfaction at the very top of their agenda in order to stand out from the competition. Others may publicly espouse such a concept, but this dealership has made sure that this philosophy is deeply embedded throughout the entire business.

The result? Despite two teething problems with the cars, we have nothing but admiration for the way in which they treated us, and have absolutely no hestitation in recommending them to anyone on the lookout for a new car. Now, is that not Customer Relationship Management at its best?

Poor service is no longer an option

Think, however, of the alternatives. Without the right attitude and putting customers at the top of your agenda, any CRM programme is bound in the end to fail. If the only difference between businesses is the way they treat their customers, then why should anyone have to put up with second-rate service?

We saw earlier that the ubiquitous *'Have a nice day!'* greeting in America soon fell into disrepute as it became formulaic in the extreme. No one believed those offering such a greeting really meant what he or she was saying. Rigid, pre-defined behaviour simply removes the 'personal' (and therefore the value of) relationships between two parties.

Genuine, heart-felt care, on the other hand, is something that people really do value and they will often pay over the odds to get it. Becoming a customer-focused company requires every aspect of the company to be customer-centric. CRM is not simply a marketing technique. It is something that has to come from the very top of an organisation and permeate systemically throughout everything the company does. Without this leaders and board first approach, CRM will fail.

Have you ever tried phoning your company as if you were a customer to gauge what they might feel? It can be quite a salutary experience. For instance, it never fails to amaze us how some organisations routinely hire temporary staff for their reception desks or switchboard, knowing full well that the very first point of contact with the customer is when first impressions are made. What do they think they are playing at? You certainly would not attempt to put an ill-prepared sales person out on the road to sell, so why make someone who does not know the business well the first contact anyone has with your business?

Now think of all the people within your organisation who

- Call centre
- Telesales
- Sales force
- Service department
- Retail outlet
- Accounts department

have some kind of contact with the real world outside, such as:

It is hardly difficult to understand that whoever the customer has to deal with in the organisation, they should get the same treatment, the same courtesies, the same level of competence and the same messages. Failing that, the customer will be left feeling confused by the mixed messages given out.
Customers should be treated as VIPs or honoured guests.

Everyone in the business needs to have the three golden CRM principles firmly embedded in their psyche:

1 *Involvement*: showing awareness of and concern for the customers' agendas and acknowledging their concerns.
2 *Respect*: of the customers, acknowledging their competences and achievements
3 *Affection*: being warm, approachable and genuinely concerned about the well being of the customer

Your front-end staff might be trained to display these emotions, but what do they experience when they deal internally, within the organisation, for the back up they need? How much involvement, respect and affection is there within your company for the front-line staff who have to deal with the customers?

Much of the way we make value judgements is based on the personality traits of the people we deal with, and it is quite clear that some people are very much more 'sympathetic' and in tune with people's needs than others. Recruiting people with the right attitude and personality is vitally important when choosing your front-line staff.

Similarly, some people are better than others in handling complex information and are able to structure their decisions based on the available facts, as well as using their intuition. These people should also be on your shopping list of customer care agents (as they are now called in the US).

The culture of an organisation

How can you cultivate an organisational culture based around the customer? Firstly, as we have already mentioned, a company that treats its own people in the way it wishes its customers to be treated, sets the agenda for everyday interaction; even without thinking, people will start behaving in a customer-centric manner. This can be enhanced and supported by incentivising structures, such as using customer-satisfaction scores to work out the organisation's profit-sharing programme. To do this, the sales force should be given incentives to retain current customers in preference to acquiring new customers. Any commission schemes the company has in place may need to be realigned to support multi-channel strategies.

Employees who see senior management behaving in a certain way are more likely to accept that behaviour and behave like that themselves, than those who are expected to behave differently from the way their bosses do. *'Don't do as I do; do as I say'* is an outmoded way of managing.

The effects of an organisational culture that is led from the top can be broken down into four areas.

1 Only by understanding the culture can employees understand the firm's current attitude to its customers and the approach to its markets. No one should be in any doubt about the standards of behaviour expected from everyone.
2 Organisational culture should also give guidance about the company's common goals and foster happy commitment to corporate values.
3 Organisational culture should be a means of steering employee behaviour towards a desired standard.
4 Organisational culture can be responsible for generating better productivity and greater effectiveness than competitors and other businesses who do not have the positive culture.

Remember, though, that it really does not matter what you do to change the culture of an organisation if you ignore the most basic rule about CRM:

> *Nothing impresses a customer like competence and care.*

And the corollary of this:

> *Nothing is more guaranteed to turn away a customer than incompetence and the lack of a sense of care.*

Customers return to businesses they like and they shun businesses where they have had a bad experience. That much is obvious. If you think of your everyday dealings with a whole raft of organisations, which ones stick in your mind? The ones that give you outstanding service (fewer than 10 per cent of those you deal with)?; or the ones offering you poor or abysmal service (again around 10 per cent); or the 'OK' ones – the 80 per cent of companies that are unmemorable with service levels that are acceptable, but nothing to write home about?

In this book we have already talked about poor service companies; and about the organisations that impress us no end and whom we would willingly return to again and again. With CRM, being good enough is no longer good enough. You and your organisation have to be the best from top to toe.

Summary

Customer care is not only about how front-end staff treat an organisation's customers. It has to be led and supported throughout the entire organisation from the highest levels.

Reward structures, leading by example and brilliant communication, are the best ways to instil a culture which encourages individual commitment to treating everyone – whether external customers or internal colleagues – by the three golden principles of Involvement, Respect and Affection.

Motivating the CRM workforce

The correct mix of skills

Getting the correct mix of skills in any organisation is difficult, but true CRM imposes extra constraints that must be identified and tackled head-on. Technical staff may be perfectly suited to having a screwdriver and a set of instructions and being told to get on with the job, but it is a sad fact that many technophiles and very focused specialists have poor interpersonal skills.

Reception staff and telephone operators, on the other hand, are usually recruited for their telephone manner, their personalities and their empathy with customers. They are not hired for their technical skills, specialist knowledge or understanding of the customer's home turf environment.

The challenge for all businesses, therefore, has to be to give front-line staff enough technical, specialist knowledge and business insight, both to understand the problems faced by customers and to come up with a solution based on the facts, while training the second rung technical and specialist staff with enough customer-friendly skills to handle customer enquiries.

We have already seen that different skills sets are needed for the different rungs of the customer enquiry escalation ladder, ranging from the less-skilled staff at the first point of contact with the outside world, to the high-level support desk where experts are brought in when all others have failed.

In general, the introduction of CRM to an organisation requires, at the very least, four types of training:

1 Customer service skills
2 Product and service skills
3 System skills
4 Team working skills

Handling customers professionally is something that can be taught. It is an attitude, and the manner in which people are treated follows the attitude. It is not enough to smile into a telephone and openly empathise with your customers. Front-line staff invariably have to deal with angry customers frustrated with what they see as incompetence in the organisation and who vent their spleen on the first person they come across representing that company. Training in knowing how to deal with such people is therefore essential, and is one of the most important skills a front-line person can possess. (For more on this subject, read *Dealing with Difficult People in a week* in this series.)

Training is essential

Fully integrating front-line people into the workings of any organisation is something that is both essential and, unfortunately, often ignored. How frequently have you contacted someone to ask about a new or oft-advertised product or service, and they seem to know even less about it than you do? What is the point of putting such people at the front line of your business? Timely training of front-line staff is essential whenever a new product or service is launched, otherwise the message the company gives out is that: (a) it is incompetent; (b) it does not value its products enough to proclaim them to its own people, let alone the outside world and (c) it does not respect or value its customers and prospective customers enough to give them good, well-trained, knowledgeable and approachable people to deal with.

With the wealth of software and other technologies that are available and being implemented in CRM-aware organisations, companies cannot afford not to train their people to use them, and refine their knowledge and interpersonal skills to beat the competition in customer relationships. Call management and knowledge tools are not cheap and, although we know that 80 per cent of people normally only use 20 per cent of the capabilities of professional word processors, this kind of complacency cannot be allowed within CRM systems if the investment is not to be totally wasted. The balance between using the technology and having well-trained people to work with, is a fine one and different in each firm.

The pressures involved in working on the front line, taking the flack from disgruntled customers and dealing with other problems, mean that social chemistry is very important and mutual comradeship is essential. Many organisations routinely engage staff in team-building events and training, in the hope that the turnover rate of staff can be lessened from the normal 30 per cent of people in call centre environments who leave within a year.

Improving service levels

In an ideal CRM world, those who interact with customers should act as catalysts for change within the organisation. Nevertheless, many companies place their front-end staff far removed from the everyday workings of the rest of the organisation – often in a remote building where interaction with the the rest of the organisation is all but impossible.

If front-end staff have little access to senior management, little will be fed back to those who can make changes and many opportunities will be lost. In fact, if there is a gulf between the customer service centre and the main part of the business, there will be a gulf between the main business and its customers. Vast amounts of effort are needed to bridge that gulf to ensure that any compromises made are not to the detriment of customer relationships.

CRM is more to do with the process, than with the system that enables that process in the first place. By failing to detail the procedures by which service levels are clearly defined, people will be inclined to make up the rules as they go along, leading to inconsistent service levels of variable quality. Furthermore, achievements against targets should be measurable if service levels are to be managed at all.

It is often said, with some justification, that a manager who spends time at a customer help desk will usually have a far greater insight into the health of the company, and by spending time on an internal help desk they will learn a great deal about staff morale and disaffection.

Try this!

Many organisations have implemented a system of internal charges, where products or services supplied by one department to another are charged as if the receiving department were an external customer. The problem with this approach if it charges internal departments for accessing help desks, is that those in need might think twice about making the call in the first place, even though the company as a whole will benefit from improved productivity.

If, instead, your organisation charged the department responsible for creating the problem in the first place, the full cost of the mistake would be borne by those who necessitated the call to the help desk. Over time, the incentive to improve standards in the poorly managed department would be inescapable. No longer could they deliver shoddy work in the expectation that the help desk would come in later to clear up the mess!

Think carefully of the implications before carrying this out; policing this can cause further problems of team breakdown if the interdepartmental communications are not so good.

Motivation by reward

When training your people to be more customer-centric, a carrot and stick approach can be used to reinforce the training messages given out. For instance, if you can introduce a system that rewards efforts for supporting specific customer-centric goals, then you must ensure that other rewards are not set at odds with this particular process.

How refreshing it is to reward critical performance and ground-breaking ideas rather than routine tasks; this positive and proactive approach will encourage the formation of a competitive edge over your competition and send out signals to the rest of the workforce that such behaviour is well valued.

In addition, you should aim to reward performance that sets a good example to others. Rapid feedback is essential if any reward system is to have any effect and, if a reward can be given publicly, it reinforces the emphasis on customer-service behaviour – not only for the person who earned the reward, but for others who see that they could be similarly rewarded for such behaviour. That, in itself, will trigger the attitudinal changes that when your business needs as a continually improving customer relationship strategy is brought into the realms of day-to-day business.

Empowerment

If you examine the main factors that influence customers' perceptions of a company, high on the list is their interaction with company staff. In a hotel, for example, guests will form the basis of their opinions on how well they are treated by doorpeople and reception staff initially, and then by restaurant (especially breakfast) staff and so on.

It follows, therefore, that service quality can be greatly enhanced by giving these people more responsibility and by empowering them with decision making, without having to pass queries back up and down the line. In this way, most problems and complaints can, and should, be prevented

before they even have a chance to appear, and the overall customer impression of the organisation is improved.

Staff training is fundamantal because some staff may become over-zealous in attempting to make amends for what might be only minor problems. Company training should be devoted to:

- Creating and encouraging staff enthusiasm
- Developing skills that allow and enable staff to attempt to solve problems
- Developing a company culture and attitude that achieves continual improvement in customer relationships, rather than one-off specific performance targets

Involving your people in decision making also improves their feelings of self-worth. It can deliver substantially lower costs since it is often the front-line staff who have the clearest picture of the procedures and can find ways of addressing them more readily than people further from the coalface.

One very successful manager used to have a notice pinned up on his wall. It read:

> *'No one has a monopoly of good ideas, not even your boss. If you think you have a good idea, I want you to tell me about it. If you think some of my ideas are rubbish, I expect you to tell me about that as well!'*

By breaking down rigid demarcations and encouraging people to believe in themselves, a successful manager can promote a proactive and service-centric culture within the organisation.

Mission statements

There are many who decry the use of mission statements in order to motivate staff. But then, rampant and often apparently disembodied slogans quoted out of context, with no feeling of the fundamentals of what the business is striving for, are bound to sound hollow.

When implementing CRM, however, short truisms can summarise what the customer team (i.e. the *whole* organisation) is trying to achieve and set a memorable objective to focus on in day-to-day work.

Here is a selection, taken from a number of different organisations. Many are repeated over and over again by different companies – which goes to prove that in the realm of CRM, the end product of complete customer satisfaction is the goal embraced by everyone.

- We put 100 per cent customer satisfaction as our overriding priority
- We will do whatever it takes to resolve a customer's problem
- We will communicate openly and readily with one another
- People should be allowed to make mistakes, just so long as they then learn from those mistakes
- Legal and/or ethical breaches will not be tolerated
- Constructive criticism should be viewed as an opportunity for improvement
- The highest standards and expectations should start with ourselves
- Looking after customers is not my job or your job; it is everyone's job

Summary

When introducing CRM to any organisation, training is absolutely essential in order to improve levels of:

- Customer service skills
- Product and service skills
- System skills
- Team working skills

Fundamentally, training will enable mind-set changes and attitudinal change, and encourage enhanced customer relationships to become the norm rather than the exception.

Front-line staff should not be so removed from the rest of the organisation that they cannot relate to the culture surrounding all other employees. The rest of the organisation should not be similarly removed from the front-line staff who act, in so many situations, as a kind of barometer of customer satisfaction. If the customers are upset or puzzled about anything, you can guarantee that the front-line staff will be the first to hear about it. Feedback on customer responses and relationships needs to be cascaded throughout the business for everyone to feel involved. Again, good communications are crucial.

By rewarding staff openly for being customer-centric and empowering them with more responsibility towards customers, the organisation will win hands down in the way it is perceived by the outside world (as well as by suppliers and partners etc.).

In motivating the CRM workforce you will automatically find that there is an improvement of motivation for all your employees. This motivation and natural appraisal of skills should culminate in becoming systemic through the company and benefit the whole organisation.

The worst thing that you can do is to identify the CRM workforce as a separate entity within the company. In the same way as all Coca Cola employees are regarded as being sales people and customer representatives, the same attitude needs to prevail throughout all companies if the CRM or call centre people are not to be regarded as working for the company but outside the main stream.

The benefits therefore of focusing on the motivation of the CRM workforce and drilling down to identify their best mix of skills can benefit the whole organisation – as long as you let it.

The improved relationships within the company and between the company and its suppliers, customers, investors etc. should mean that a more positive attitude should prevail with greater opportunities for business growth and creativity as a natural outcome.

Sometimes the use of a mission statement or two, emblazoned over the walls or on notice boards, will help to bring the workforce behind the arrow head and will show the commitment of senior management to the aim of being a totally customer-centric company. Furthermore, a simple card by each telephone with the legend 'Show Time!' on it can uplift the approach to every phone call.

Implementation and summary

It has often been said that British people would rather suffer in silence than make a fuss about badly cooked restaurant food, oxidised wine or the appalling state of the railways.

All that has been changing as internationalism and globalisation affects every area of business and stereotypical British calmness makes way for the, perhaps, more vocal attributes of other countries.

Given the many demands of customer relationship management, pulling together all the disparate strands of CRM across an entire organisation is something not to be left to the faint-hearted. Strategy, tenacity and determination are essential if you are to achieve the goals for your business.

We have already talked about the change of culture and attitude needed within a company. However, one of the biggest headaches is the integration of different systems and different ways of doing things between various departments, not to mention between different companies if mergers or acquisitions force the need for such integration.

It is not enough to adopt the goal of becoming customer-centric and sit back while your staff then get on with it. That would be as useful as letting everyone read the first two pages of a book on empowerment and then watching them break every rule. Communications, information gathering and dissemination, and business processes all need to be knitted together in addition to the complex technical problems associated with them all. And, equally as important, all the people in the business need to be enthused and educated to provide – what will become essential for a company to survive – excellent relationships with customers.

Of these, information, for example, drives the business, but it comes from many different sources. Newer systems designs allow data to be 'interrogated' and understood, regardless of what form the data first appeared in. Alternatively, data can be processed in its original incarnation and then imported to an all-seeing, all-encompassing knowledge base, structured around relational databases and so-called fuzzy logic, which looks for clues within the data.

Even on the human level, business processes need to harmonise. If a warehouse runs out of a critical component, for example, it will affect a customer order. If the factory, warehouse and customer service desk are unable to communicate adequately, how is CRM ever to be achieved? Getting everyone behind the arrow head of change and up to speed on the use of the technology, as well as making sure that the corporate attitude is right is not easy and needs investment in time, energy and money.

The enterprise-wide and cultural implications of implementing a CRM strategy are far-reaching. It will affect logistics, sales, marketing, relations with suppliers and partners, finances, internal relationships and, of course, the whole reason you implemented it in the first place – your relationship with your customers and prospective customers.

Although the process of getting different systems to 'talk to one another' is an IT issue, the whole strategy is a business issue which the board and the business managers need to comprehend – even if only the principles involved – before considering embarking on a major CRM project. Too many companies expect that investing in IT systems will guarantee success and they are invariably disappointed. CRM requires a holistic view of the organisation – both inside and out.

Implementing IT roll-outs of CRM software is something that regularly overruns both budgets and time-scales; but this is nothing compared to the amount of resources that need to be allocated for training, consultancy and business process re-engineering.

Putting it into practice

Before starting to implement CRM, the project should be scoped in great detail. If expectations are to be met, time spent on this crucial stage is essential. In this way, realistic expectations of implementation, training and projected achievement can be raised. Milestones can be set so that everyone in the business knows the position on the route map and the achievement of everyone within that.

Board level enthusiasm and 'buy-in' is also vital and many companies allocate a director to steer the project through the top-most levels. Buy-in from each affected department (i.e. every department) is also necessary and representatives from across the organisation need to sit in on the steering committee and cascade regular feedback of the progress.

Most CRM projects (like most large projects), however well managed, run into unforeseen problems, and it would be foolish not to allow slippage in both the time-scales and budgets. A contingency budget should be included at the very least, so that the project does not fail at the eleventh hour because of lack of funds. A series of contingency plans should also be drawn up to ensure that if there are points of failure, there is a holding position the company can use until the problems have been sorted out.

One area that inevitably leads to misunderstandings and resistance is when activity is tracked in an area that might not have been monitored before and staff feel they are being spied upon and measured against various yardsticks. Instead, people need to understand and feel that, with better information at their finger tips, they will be able to achieve much more than they ever did and that by automating mundane processes, their jobs should become more interesting and enjoyable.

Remember, too, that organisations which fail to make allowance for adequate staff training – including refresher courses – may be throwing away much of their initial investment.

The impact of CRM

Most companies discussing the introduction of some level of CRM will want to know the payback for incorporating this philosophy into their workplace and creating major changes with the way things have been done for so long. What is really achievable? And what is the return on investment (ROI) likely to be?

ROI is something that is hotly debated because boards are not willing to sign a blank cheque for something that may or may not bring solid returns to the bottom line.

Unfortunately and short-sightedly, many companies use performance standards to measure their return on investment, such as the number of calls being handled in a call centre. As we have already seen, this is a crude measure of success. The real value lies in delivering the improved benefits each customer wants, in order to encourage them to return again and again, thereby costing the company less in real terms and delivering more in profitability for a lower overall expenditure.

One way to look at things is to identify the difference between what a customer is spending now and what they could be spending if CRM were to be implemented. Some questions in particular need to be asked:

- How could information gathering be improved?
- Do we encourage customers to buy other products from us, rather than just the ones they sought initially?
- Are we losing customers to our competitors because

> they handle them better?
> - Do we know enough about our clients?
> - Do our clients know what they want to know about us?
> - Do our clients complain about any particular aspect of what we do?

Only by answering questions like these can organisations really get to grips with the ROI provided by CRM and establish real and quantifiable business benefits.

There is another measure that organisations need to use if they want to know how effective their CRM strategy really is. They should ask their customers!

ON A SCALE OF 1:10 HOW WOULD YOU RATE OUR SURVEY TECHNIQUE?

Organisations should:

- Identify satisfaction criteria for each market segment
- Survey a valid sample of these customers in order to provide a score for each of the criteria, using a reputable independent survey company
- Survey a valid sample of people who are not customers (but are customers of a competitor) to try to assess a benchmark for that particular segment of the market – again with an independent company so that the information gathered is not skewed by biased questions
- Compare their own scores with the industry benchmarks to identify (and then put to rights) anything that it discovers is lacking in its own offerings or service

The final piece of the jigsaw is to establish effective monitoring systems that report back to the relevant personnel and thereby give the correct amount of feedback to those who can use it effectively for the good of the organisation.

From first principles to roll-out

To summarise the whole process, we need to start with a customer strategy if CRM is to succeed. Each customer has different needs and the trick of successful CRM is to divide the customers into different groups, ranging from the most profitable to the least lucrative (who may not be worth targeting at all). From these segments you can determine which groups are worth spending time and money on to develop.

Eight questions need to be addressed to ensure that you are on the right track in terms of designing your CRM proposition.

1 What must we do to earn greater customer loyalty?
2 How much customisation needs be undertaken to ensure profitability for the strategy?
3 What extra value will be added by increasing customer loyalty, and how does this vary between the different segments?
4 How can resources be devoted to CRM at the present time?
5 What do our customers like about us the most?
6 What do our customers hate about us?
7 What do our customers want from us that we do not already do or provide?
8 What can be done to improve relationships with customers without any spending on technology?

This last question is important because, according to many firms and research groups in the US, between one-third and one-half of CRM projects fail. The reasons why they fail are manifold, but invariably it is because many company executives simply do not understand what they are implementing or are not fully engaged in the pursuit of customer satisfaction.

Bearing in mind that it can easily take up to 24 months for a CRM system to be fully implemented across an organisation, it appears that many executives are simply too impatient to see concrete results. As a result, they make a number of mistakes, the most common of which include:

- Implementing CRM before thinking it through properly and creating a customer strategy
- Implementing CRM before changing the mind-set and attitude of an organisation
- Assuming that CRM has to be technology intensive and that the more technological solutions are implemented, the better and more foolproof it is
- Stalking and annoying potential customers, rather than wooing them with good service and great products *that they actually want*

Simply put, while technology is a powerful facilitator for CRM, that is all it is. IT is one of the enablers. Get the strategy right first and investigate the technology afterwards. If you don't, you might find that your CRM tools result in you losing customers, rather than building customer loyalty.

Wrapping up

It is a complete fallacy to think that companies will have an edge over the competition simply because they are internet-based or because they are using the latest technologies or management fashions. If all they do is re-engineer what is already being done, techology will not benefit them.

For companies to compete effectively in the future in the attempt to meet customer expectations and manage customer relations brilliantly, they must ensure that their customers are central to everything they do. All other 'strategies' are doomed to failure.

SUN

MON

TUE

WED

THU

FRI

SAT

For information

on other

IN A **WEEK** titles

go to

www.inaweek.co.uk